Our American Family™

I Am African American

Ruth Turk

The Rosen Publishing Group's
PowerKids Press™
New York

To Len—the best husband and research assistant an author ever h

Published in 1997 by The Rosen Publishing Group, Inc.
29 East 21st Street, New York, NY 10010

First Edition

Book Design: Erin McKenna

Photo Credits: Cover © Dennie Cody/FPG International Corp.; photo illustration © Icon Comm/FPG International Corp.; p. 4 © Arthur Tilley/FPG International Corp.; p. 7 © Geopress/H. Armstrong Roberts, Inc.; p. 8 © Bettmann; p. 11 © Corbis-Bettmann; p. 12 © UPI/Corbis-Bettmann; p. 15 © Fred Phillips/Impact Visuals; p. 16 © Christopher Smith/Impact Visuals; p. 19 © J. Graham/H. Armstrong Roberts, Inc.; p. 20 © Terry Qing/FPG International Corp.

Turk, Ruth.
    I am African American / by Ruth Turk.
        p.   cm. — (Our American family)
    Includes index.
    Summary: An African American child talks briefly about various elements of his heritage, such as slavery, family traditions, foods, and clothing as well as about outstanding African Americans in history.
    ISBN 0-8239-5007-7
    1. Afro-Americans—Juvenile literature.   [1. Afro-Americans]   I. Title. II. Series.
E185.T85 ¯1997
973'.0496073—dc21   96-5392
                                                                      CIP
                                                                      AC

Manufactured in the United States of America

Contents

This Is My Family

My name is Jesse. I am an African American. I live in a part of New York City called Queens. I am in the fourth grade. My father works as a lawyer and my mother is a music teacher. My parents tell me stories about my **ancestors** (AN-ses-terz), such as my great-great-great grandparents. They came to this country from Africa. My great-great-great grandparents were **slaves** (SLAYVZ). They worked on a **plantation** (plan-TAY-shun) in South Carolina.

◀ Many African American families believe it is important to remember their African ancestors.

5

Africa

Africa is a huge **continent** (KON-tih-nent). It is made up of 40 countries with dry deserts, wet rain forests, and busy cities. Some Africans live in homes on the plains or in the forests. Others live in houses or large buildings in the cities. Many Africans belong to different groups, or peoples. Each people has its own language and customs.

African peoples have rich **traditions** (truh-DISH-unz) of art, religion, and music. Many of their ideas have spread all over the world.

This is the city of Conakry, in the country of Guinea. Cities are different all over Africa. Some are big and ▶ modern, while others are smaller and more rural.

Slavery

Beginning in the 1700s, many Africans were brought to America against their will and sold as slaves. Many of them worked on plantations in the South. Slaves were considered the property of the people who bought and sold them. They were often beaten and forced to work long hours with little rest or food. Many slaves escaped. Others were helped by people who wanted to **abolish** (uh-BOL-ish) slavery. My great-great-great grandparents escaped on a boat going to New York, where slavery had already been abolished.

Slavery was a cruel and inhumane system of labor. Millions of Africans were brought to the United States as slaves. They were treated as things, not people.

Harriet Tubman

My mother taught me about Harriet Tubman. She was a slave on a plantation in Maryland. She worked in the fields from sunrise to sunset. Her owner was very mean to her and the other slaves. But Harriet escaped from the plantation in 1849 on the Underground Railroad. This was a network of people who helped slaves along an escape route from the South to the North. Harriet returned to the South many times as part of the Underground Railroad to help other slaves. She led more than 300 slaves to freedom.

Harriet Tubman worked bravely with others on the Underground Railroad to bring ▶ slaves to freedom in the North.

Martin Luther King, Jr.

Until the late 1960s, black and white people were separated by law. They couldn't share the same buses, restaurants, or even the same public water fountains. This separation was called **segregation** (seh-greh-GAY-shun). African Americans were treated as second class citizens. Like many others, Martin Luther King, Jr. knew that this **racism** (RAY-sizm) was wrong. He fought for equal rights. By 1965, laws were passed stating that everyone is equal. My family admires Martin Luther King, Jr. very much.

◀ Martin Luther King, Jr.'s powerful speeches affected many people. But some didn't agree with his beliefs. He was killed in 1968 by someone who didn't agree with him.

13

Kwanzaa

Kwanzaa is an African American holiday that was started in 1966 by a teacher named Maulana Karenga. It falls on December 26th each year, and lasts for seven days. Kwanzaa celebrates the peoples of Africa, honors our past, and reminds us of our present and future in this world. The family is also very important during Kwanzaa. My family and I decorate the house in black, green, yellow, and red, the colors that symbolize Africa. Our family members give each other gifts. On the last day of Kwanzaa, we don't eat until sunset. Then we have a big meal together.

A candle is lit on each day of Kwanzaa. Each candle represents a different principle, or idea, relating to the ▶ importance of being an African American.

Traditional Clothing

On special occasions, some African Americans wear traditional African clothes. During Kwanzaa, my mother wears a **bubba** (BUB-buh). Other women might braid their hair in **cornrows** (KORN-rowz). My father wears a **dashiki** (dash-EE-kee), or a long shirt. Men also wear **kofis** (KO-feez) on their heads and beads around their necks.

For my birthday, my parents gave me a shirt made of *kente* cloth. *Kente* is a beautiful material from the country of Ghana in Africa.

◀ These men wear colorful dashikis and kofis during special celebrations.

17

Soul Food

As slaves, my great-great-great grandparents did not have a lot of food to eat. So they used spices and their knowledge of African cooking to make new dishes, called soul food. Today, when our family eats together, we eat some of the same foods that my ancestors did, such as corn bread, black-eyed peas, and **corn pone** (KORN pohn). My mom says she remembers eating soul food at her grandparents' house. She has taught me how to make some of my favorite dishes.

When my relatives come to visit, they all bring different dishes to eat. We enjoy ▶ sharing soul food together.

Sharing Our Music

Using African **rhythms** (RIH-thumz), African Americans invented new kinds of music. They include jazz, **spirituals** (SPEER-it-choo-uls), gospel, soul, blues, and rock and roll music. These are now enjoyed all over the world. There are hundreds of famous African American musicians. Today, singers like Whitney Houston use African American music forms in their modern music. Rap is also another form of music that has roots in African and African American **culture** (KUL-cher).

◀ Jazz is one form of music that is strongly influenced by African culture.

21

I Am Proud

My parents go to work and I go to school, but we always find the time to eat dinner together. Sometimes we talk about our ancestors and the days of slavery. After dinner we might look at family pictures in our big photo album. I want to learn more about where my great-great-great grandparents came from. Last year, my cousin traveled to Mali, a country in West Africa. She said she might someday take me to another country called Kenya in East Africa. I hope I get to go.

22

Glossary

abolish (uh-BOL-ish) To get rid of.

ancestor (AN-ses-ter) A relative who lived before you.

bubba (BUB-buh) A long African dress.

continent (KON-tih-nent) A large land mass.

corn pone (KORN pohn) Cornbread that is made without milk or eggs and is baked or fried.

cornrows (KORN-rowz) Hair that is divided into small sections and braided close to the head.

culture (KUL-cher) The beliefs, customs, and religions of a group of people.

dashiki (dash-EE-kee) A long African shirt.

kofi (KO-fee) An African hat.

plantation (plan-TAY-shun) A large farm or estate, usually in the South.

racism (RAY-sizm) The mistaken belief that one race is better than another.

rhythm (RIH-thum) To repeat a beat in pattern.

segregation (seh-greh-GAY-shun) Separation by race.

slave (SLAYV) A person who is forced to work for someone else.

spiritual (SPEER-it-choo-ul) Of or having to do with the spirit.

tradition (truh-DISH-un) A way of doing something that is passed down from parent to child.

23

Index

24